NLP

How To Control People's Minds, Induce Hypnosis In Them, And Influence Them With Your Persuasion And Hypnosis Skills

(How To Recognize And Avoid Being Manipulated By Dark Psychology, As Well As Who Practices It)

AchimSpindler

TABLE OF CONTENT

Comprehending The Personalities Of The Dark Triad 1

The Use Of NLP Strategies And Methods 5

Different Hypnotic Language Patterns Include The Following: 12

The Many Lines Of Connection 20

The Secret To Turning Negative Feelings Into Positive Ones 40

An Introduction To Nlp 49

Using NLP To Erase Unpleasant Memories 61

Where You Ought To Make Use Of Nlp 69

It Is Completely Dependent Upon Your Conduct. 83

NLP Fundamentals 96

Techniques For Manipulating Someone's Emotions 115

The Drawbacks Of Being A Manipulator 129

Continuing Education And Training 134

The Use Of NLP In Treatment And Beyond ... 140

Comprehending The Personalities Of The Dark Triad

There is not one single, overarching medical diagnostic that can be used to categorize all instances of deviant personalities that fall within the purview of dark psychology. There are a variety of ways in which dark psychology might show itself in the mental and behavioral make-up of an individual. There is no clear line that can be drawn between different aberrant personality types in an absolute sense. Multiple manifestations of dark psychology are likely to be present in the personality of many deviant individuals who have major dark psychology elements.

Psychopathy in a sentence.

Psychopathy is a mental disorder that is characterized by a number of identifying characteristics, including antisocial behavior, amorality, an inability to develop empathy, inability to establish meaningful personal relationships, extreme egocentricity, and recidivism, which is defined as repeated violations of rules as a result of an apparent inability to learn from the consequences of earlier transgressions. Psychopathy is defined as a mental disorder with several identifying characteristics. Antisocial behavior, on the other hand, is described as behavior that is centered upon the purpose of breaching formal and/or informal standards of social conduct via criminal action or by acts of personal, private protest or resistance, both of which are directed against other individuals and society in general.

The conduct known as egocentrism occurs when a person views themselves as the focal point of the world, or at the very least, of the majority of the social and political action taking place at any one time.

Empathy is the capacity to experience and comprehend situations, thoughts, feelings, and beliefs from the point of view of another individual. It is often regarded as one of the fundamental psychological components necessary for the establishment of fruitful, long-lasting partnerships.

The distinction between immorality and amorality cannot be overstated. An action that goes against the moral standards that have been established is considered immoral. This sort of individual takes comfort in their acts with the assumption that they will comprehend that their actions are objectionable from a moral sense, if not legally. This expectation is based on the fact that their actions violate the rights of others. On the other side, amoral psychology refers to a school of thought that denies the existence of universally accepted moral standards. If they do, then their opinions are worthless when it comes to choosing between several courses of action. Therefore, a person demonstrating psychopathy may be capable of doing horrifying crimes that inflict immense psychological and physical damage and never realize that what they have done is wrong, despite the fact that they have caused such trauma to others. Worse than that, persons who exhibit indicators of psychopathy often deteriorate over time because they are unable to see the connection between the difficulties in their own lives and the lives of others in the world around them and the harmful and destructive activities that they do.

The Use OfNLP Strategies And Methods

One may argue that self-assurance is one of the most important qualities that a person should strive to cultivate in themselves. It might be difficult for a person to see clearly the steps leading to success if they do not have a strong sense of confidence, a high level of faith in themselves, or a firm conviction in their talents. This is due to the fact that a person's confidence in himself determines how far that individual is willing to go to achieve the objective that he has dreamed of. Castale offered advice on how to boost one's self-assurance by making use of the many NLP approaches. To begin, he walks his readers through the process of visualizing what a really confident person looks like and how they behave. Then, he instructs the audience to go back on a time in their life when they were brimming with self-assurance and belief in themselves, and he encourages them to dwell on that memory for a bit. Castale then challenges his audience to see themselves as being completely self-assured in every endeavor or activity they now partake in or want to participate in at some point in the future. When we examine simply the steps that Castale supplied his reader for adopting NLP approaches, we come to the fact that the search for ways to enhance one's personality and intellect requires a significant amount of mental effort on the part of the individual.

As was noted earlier, Non-Linguistic Programming (NLP) plays an important part in the development of the communication process in addition to its function in boosting confidence. Building rapport, knowing how to communicate successfully via the use of suitable and right language, and even responding to criticism are all examples of communication skills that can be developed and improved upon. Castale is of the opinion that developing rapport is one of the most important steps in the process of personal growth. This is due to the fact that rapport is the bond that binds us all together.

NLP was formerly recognized by Modern Psychology Magazine as a school of thinking that have the potential to become the most significant factor in the evolution and development of the whole human race. This might be linked to the fact that NLP is able to be learnt and utilized in such a way that it can improve a large number of facets of an individual's life. Training and even treatment for a variety of issues have been accomplished via the application of NLP. These concerns may be broken down into three primary categories: the resolution of problems, the development of innovative solutions, and the attainment of one's goals. What NLP accomplishes in the aforementioned categories is essentially assist people examine themselves to find out their liabilities, and then it provides ways to overcome those hindrances so that the participating people will become better persons who are capable of achieving their objectives.

In light of the fact that NLP is beneficial to the development of other parts of personality, let us now analyze its link to the process of intellectual learning and the ways in which it might potentially help an individual's learning capacity to advance at a faster rate.

In contrast to the traditional learning model, which consists of oral examinations, the memorization of facts, and instructions that are solely based on the text books that are used by the school, the NLP learning strategies suggest better and more effective ways of learning so that the students will not simply regurgitate knowledge that has been passed on from one generation to another, but rather will comprehend every detail about that fact that they were taught. In addition, learning techniques often incorporate practical application of knowledge in order to boost the efficiency of the learning process. Visualization and metaphors, as well as reframing and anchoring, are some of the additional learning tools that the new field of NLP has presented.

The term "visualization" alludes to the fact that it is comprised of several different actions that make extensive use of many perceiving senses. For instance, pupils in a badminton lesson would understand the distinction between a smash and a drop if they had really seen how to execute the many skills required for the sport. On the other hand, making use of metaphors paves the path for students' thought processes that extend beyond what they are really being taught. A cockroach that lives in dirty rubbish is the subject of a poem that is discussed in a literary class, which is an example of the usage of metaphors as a tactic for instructing students. The whole class becomes involved in the conversation when one student raises the possibility that roaches may be a metaphor for selfish politicians, and they try to figure out how the symbolism could be conceivable. The student who raised the possibility was called on to explain their concept. An person is not constrained to a notion that is presented to him because of the usage of metaphors; rather, he is given the opportunity to explore and learn a whole other way of thinking.

Altering one's perspective on an idea or circumstance is the focus of the technique known as "reframing." For instance, if he finds himself in a challenging circumstance, he will reframe the problem and work to find a constructive solution so that he may escape the difficulties. When applied to the process of education, it may manifest itself in scenarios such as the following: a student believes that his test will be challenging; nevertheless, he later revises this belief and believes that he will be able to pass the examination with flying colors. Because our whole body reacts to how our brain reacts to a certain circumstance, this strategy is one that many individuals find to be beneficial.

Last but not least, anchoring is a teaching method that involves an instructor presenting a fresh concept to his students at precisely the time when those students are in the most receptive condition possible. Students have a far better chance of being able to recollect the information that they have studied if they are given several opportunities to practice applying what they have learned.

Different Hypnotic Language Patterns Include The Following:

The following list provides twenty of the most powerful hypnotic language patterns, along with some examples of how each of these patterns should be used. This is done in a manner that ensures that it will not only be useful to the seller but will also have a favorable influence on the seller's connection with the buyer. Specifically, this is done to guarantee that the seller will make a profit.

The greater the amount of, the greater the:

If you communicate with the consumer using phrases such as "The more you think about it, the more you will want it" or "The more you use this product, the more you will wonder how you lived so long without it," you will be able to entice them into reevaluating the worth of the product you are selling. People who are on the fence about something are the ideal candidates for this strategy.

When you ___, then you ___: "When you get around to trying this product even just once, then you will see how perfect it is for you!" alternatively, "When you realize how many different ways it can simplify your life, you will be so happy that you made the decision to purchase it!" since of the way these lines are worded, the consumer will consider the possibility of giving the product a try, and as a result, he will be more inclined to make a purchase since it provides him with a potential opportunity for the future.

It is important to keep in mind that __: This is yet another wonderful approach to subtly convince a buyer. When you say things to him like "You should remember that this offer is only for today," or "You should remember that you are one of our only few privileged customers snatching this deal...", he will be more likely to make the buy right away. In this approach, the consumer is put under a little bit of pressure to make a choice more quickly.

I'm sure the following questions are on your mind:

This phrase can be used in a variety of contexts by the seller. Some examples include the following: "I know you are wondering how this product will be useful to you, and I have just the answer for that..." or "I know you are wondering if this is worth the price it, but let me tell you that it is actually a steal because it has amazing features such as...". The customer's questions regarding the product are answered before the client ever has a chance to ask them, and the vendor is able to place further emphasis on the product's applications.

You may say something like, "Maybe you need to give this product an opportunity!" or "Maybe you are concerned about the price, but don't you worry because this product..." if you're not sure what to do with this goods. The customer will have the impression that he is being given a chance if he is first presented with potential outcomes and then provided with potential remedies to those outcomes. There are a variety of applications for this phrase. Another way to put it is, "Maybe you are worried now, but wait till you get to use it!"

And as you do this, so you do that: "And as you buy this, don't forget to inform your friends, so that you can all enjoy this product," or "And as you begin to have an issue, give us a call, so that you can have it resolved in no time!"

This tactic fosters a healthy and long-lasting connection between the customer and the seller by providing the former with reassurance over the latter's purchase.

simply __because__.

"Just because you haven't had the opportunity to use this product up to this point doesn't mean you can't have it now..." or "Only because you are my most loyal customer, I am going to give you an additional discount..." are both phrases that may be used to persuade someone to buy something from you.

This term lends itself well to a wide variety of inventive applications. In the first example, the term is used to suggest that the problem with the client is of lower relevance when compared to the chance to try something new. However, in the second example, the word 'because' is used to convey that the issue with the customer is of the utmost importance.

If it implies __: "If it means you will even consider buying this product, then I am willing to help you understand it further." Before the buyer makes a choice about making the purchase, this will demonstrate to the buyer that the seller is truly concerned and is prepared to spend the time necessary to ensure that the buyer feels at ease with the situation. This helps to create stronger relationships with customers.

It's a fact, it's a fact, it's a fact, an indirect suggestion, and a tag question.

Putting a question at the conclusion of a few thoughts and recommendations prompts the brain to digest the information in a condensed fashion and do an analysis of the complete scenario. The question that is posed at the very end brings closure to the intriguing possibility, as well as leaves an indelible mark on the mind. Because of this, there is an increased possibility that the client will agree. Take, for instance, the phrase "This product is affordable. It has a guarantee attached to it. In addition to that, there is a refund policy. Buying it won't hurt you in any way, shape, or form in any way. The question then becomes, "Why not give it a chance?" After providing a rundown of the product's most appealing qualities, the salesperson should pose questions to the potential buyer that are difficult for them to decline.

If the vendor adds a personal touch to his statement, the customer is instantly pulled to believing him immediately. I wouldn't advise you to __ because __: If the seller adds a personal touch to his statement, the customer is automatically drawn to believing him immediately. I would say something to the effect of, "I wouldn't tell you to buy this product if I didn't trust it because I know regret is the last thing you expect," or "I would not tell you to make an impulsive decision because your satisfaction comes first." if I didn't trust the product, I wouldn't encourage you to buy it.

The Many Lines Of Connection

Because perception plays such an important part in both the theory and practice of NLP, it is essential that students have a comprehensive understanding of the function that perceptual modalities play. In NLP, we talk about five different perceptual modalities total: three main, two secondary, and one tertiary. The three most important ones are one's ability to see, hear, and feel things. It is common practice to regard the gustatory and olfactory modalities to be connected to the kinesthetic one. These may be shortened to VAKOG if necessary.

The things that people see, hear, feel, taste, and smell are all ways in which they obtain perceptual information. After going through this process of filtering, these perceptions will have an effect on the subject's internal representation, state, behavior, and physiology.

Taking into account one's chosen mode of communication

One of the first things that a student of practitioner training learns is how to identify the mode or channel of communication that a certain individual is most comfortable with. This is the same as stating that despite the fact that all five channels are accessible, the typical preference of a person is to communicate via only one of them. For instance, when it comes to learning a difficult work, some individuals would rather be taught how to do it, while others would prefer to be given an in-depth explanation, and still others won't learn the task at all until they are able to do it on their own. These individuals are classified as kinesthetic, auditory, and visual learners, respectively.

It's possible that you missed one more item that I mentioned in the previous sentence. I said that practically everyone has a communication channel that is more to their liking. However, it is subject to alter when placed under stressful circumstances. During a crisis, a person who is typically more visual or auditory may swiftly switch to becoming more kinesthetic. Alternatively, an auditory one might become more kinesthetic. For example, a slow-talking kinesthetic person may have a tendency to place an emphasis on the precision of verbal communication when they are anxious, but a visual person may emotionally seize up and slow down their speech when they feel threatened.

In the beginning, I was also instructed that persons who have a certain modal preference may pick their employment in accordance with that desire. It's possible that a hard-charging corporate executive is more of a visual learner, while an announcer on the radio or a teacher in a classroom would be more auditory, and a florist, chef, or massage therapist would be more kinesthetic.

If you pay attention to how often certain predicates appear, you may also gather information on favored modes of operation. Words like "see," "demonstrate," and "show" point to a person who is more visual, "explain," "tell," and "relate" point to someone who is more auditory, while "feel" and "sense" point to someone who is more kinesthetic. In addition to this, you will encounter folks who often comment that something just smells or stinks. They learn via their sense of smell. Or, if they claim that something gives them an unpleasant aftertaste, we might conclude that they are learning via their gustatory sense.

Take note of how individuals stand, particularly their posture, as well as how they gesture and communicate. A person who communicates visually will often talk more quickly and gesture with their hands at a chest or higher level. An auditory person will talk more slowly and carefully, and their gestures will be focused more in the waist and chest area. The kinesthetic person will talk at a pace that is somewhat slower than the others because they are always focused in maintaining contact with their emotions and gestures below the waist level.

Why should we care about this? In the next book in this series, which is called Developing Instant Rapport, I will talk about the significance of establishing rapport with another person as well as the value of pacing and guiding them. It is essential to your success in these areas that you understand the manner in which they like to communicate. The advice given by NLP instructors is that you should meet your topic inside the framework of their model of the world. If they live in a kinesthetic environment and you like to take in information visually, then you are at an immediate disadvantage. If, on the other hand, you can figure out how to meet them in their model and actually speak their language, you will be able to guide them to a better functioning condition or to perfection in installation.

What I've just started talking about is how important it is for you to be flexible. The Law of Requisite Variety is considered to be one of the most important laws in NLP. Basically, what this means is that "the element of the system that possesses the most flexibility will serve as a catalyst for that system." It is necessary for you to demonstrate behavioral flexibility if you wish to be a transformational catalyst in another person's life and work as a therapist, coach, or trainer. If you are able to change your expressions, which are viewed by your subject, to fit with how they want to be connected with, then you will discover that you connect with them more quickly. This is something to keep in mind while thinking about preferred communication modalities. Nevertheless, this does not mean that there will never be a period when you find yourself wishing to switch up your look. After you have established a connection, it is sometimes required for you to be adaptable in order to initiate the process of change in the topic that you are discussing. As both this book and the series continue, further conversation will be had on this topic.

Obtaining Permission to Borrow

The practice of borrowing authority is yet another illustration of supposing the existence of social proof. In most cases, it is ideal to employ an authoritative individual or a group of people that your audience is familiar with and respects as a source of information. The unconsciously held beliefs of your audience will then confirm that your assertion is correct.

7.) Oak fountain pens, like the one I have, are favored among CEOs of companies in the Fortune 500 who use fountain pens.

Take note of what you are doing here: you are establishing a connection between the notion of Fortune 500 CEOs and the product that you are selling. Every individual will have a unique conception of what it means to be the CEO of one of the Fortune 500 companies, and this will be something that is significant to them.

Additionally, it is essential to take note that you are not being dishonest in any way. Even if you are inadvertently suggesting that CEOs of Fortune 500 companies make use of your product, you are still establishing a relationship between your product and the CEOs of those companies. When using Hypnotic Language Patterns, we never want to be dishonest at any point. You are just stating that CEOs of Fortune 500 companies utilize a product that is comparable to yours, and your audience will infer the connection between the two from this.

8.) Since hefty fountain pens are more sturdy, scientists choose ones like mine, which are heavy. This is why they use them.

Again, the audience will be unconsciously making connections between your product and this nebulous category of people who call themselves "scientists." When your consumer buys the product, they will genuinely convince themselves that they are purchasing the thing because scientists utilize this specific product. This will be a justification for them to purchase the product. They will persuade themselves that it is supported by science, and they will claim that the reason they are making the purchase is because of this.

The Pattern of the Swing

Negative anchors are the opposite of positive anchors in this context. These are the things that set us out on the path to behaviors that are limiting and emotional states that are unpleasant. There are certain foods that have the ability to send us into an eating spree so quickly that we don't even realize we're doing it until the last bite of ice cream has been consumed. It's possible that the intimidating sound of weights falling in the gym may cause us to cancel the training we had planned for ourselves. If your spouse continues to insult you in the same way that they have for the previous eight years, you may find that hearing the insult causes you to lose all of your lucidity as the argument becomes more absurd.

It is essential that we do an audit of the negative anchors that are present in our lives since they have the potential to be much more influential than their good counterparts. Specifically, any negative anchors that connect directly into our most essential aspirations or life goals must be recognized as serious dangers and dealt with in accordance with the severity of the harm they pose. They prevent us from being the persons we want to be as well as the people we are now.

As is the case with any other significant shift, we need to start by making a clear acknowledgment of the negative anchor. As a result of the fact that we often aren't conscious of the event or stimulus that sets off a pattern of behavior or thinking, this stage may be tough and calls for intentional introspection.

Asking yourself what behaviors in your life are the most destructive is a good place to start. Do you find it difficult to stick to your eating plan? Do you often fail to complete the exercises that you have planned? Do you put things off till later, giving up when you're faced with what seems like an insurmountable challenge? Do you procrastinate when your job gets overwhelming?

Start at the unfavorable result and work your way backwards through the chain of events. What occurred only a moment before this action was taken? What about earlier than that? And what about the moment just before to that? Carry on working your way backwards until you find the very first action that kicks off a chain reaction of occurrences.

Consider the case of someone who has trouble maintaining their regular gym attendance. You may be able to follow the sequence of events that led up to your most recent missed exercise all the way back to the moment when you touched the strap on your gym bag. You could remember that when you went to pick it up, a sudden recollection of the amount of effort it took to go to the gym, the misery of pushing through your exercise, and the journey home afterward came to your mind. Your mind made the decision that the reward was not worth the effort, and when you finally let go of the gym bag, you felt a mixture of failure and relief at the same time. We want to train people to have a different response when they go to retrieve their gym bag.

The neurolinguistic programming has to be rewired such that when you touch the strap of the gym bag, a surge of excitement travels through your body. Your thoughts immediately leap to the sense of accomplishment you will have after completing a strenuous exercise, the sensation of serenity and endorphins pouring through your body while you recuperate on the sofa that evening, and how well rested you will feel following a night of restful sleep in the morning. The overnight bag has all of a sudden turned into a factor that contributes to favorable results. The swish pattern is an instrument that will be used in the process of rewiring the neurolinguistic programming in your brain. It is a strong strategy, comparable to the tests in operant conditioning that Pavlov conducted, that allows you to replace your mental connections with an action. You just need around 10 minutes of your undivided attention and some mental inventiveness to complete it.

Get all of your thoughts out of the way and concentrate on recreating the occurrence that sets off the difficult chain of subsequent events (this is what we discovered only a minute ago). Imagine it in as much detail as you can. Imagine that you are looking at your hand as it reaches out to grab the strap of the gym bag, then you are pulling it up and feeling the weight of it tugging on your arm. This is the decisive moment; now is the time to rethink what will take place in the future.

Create a crystal clear vision of yourself enjoying all of the good results of your chosen activity and place it in the bottom right-hand corner of your mental image. Jump forward to the pride, contentment, physical wellness, and well-rested sensation that you will have as a result of your training. Make this as clear and distinct as the mental picture that triggered the response, but keep it tucked away in the back of your mind. Now imagine that it is becoming smaller and smaller until it is tucked away in the corner and is only just discernible. We are drawing it back as if it were connected to a rubber band in order to get this optimistic vision ready to be forcefully launched into the forefront of your mind's eye.

Now, while keeping the clarity of the picture of the trigger in your mind, be ready to let go of the rubber band that has been holding back the result. Allow the trigger picture, which is the gym bag, to spin out of your range of vision at the same quick pace as it rushes forward and takes over your field of view. You want the experience of picking up your gym bag to immediately transition into the happiness you'll feel after your exercise. This is what you want to happen. After you've reached this level of contentment, you should cleanse your thoughts. Repeat this practice a few times, at least ten times, making each subsequent visualization more vivid than the one before it, until you begin to feel that the very thought of the strap of the gym bag contacting your palm immediately sends a charge of pleasure through both your mind and your body.

If we've done the workout properly and enough times, the sensation you get when you take up your gym bag for the next time will be completely different from what it was before. A surge of excitement will go through you as you begin your pursuit of the treasures that are waiting for you. On your drive to the gym, you'll be saying prayers that the traffic lights will be green. Your exercise is about to take on a whole new level of intensity because to you. And this is how we establish strong habits that set us up for success in life - by creating expectations of the good consequences that will follow from our actions. As you can see, making use of positive anchors may have a profoundly transformative effect on one's life.

The Secret To Turning Negative Feelings Into Positive Ones

You are aware that you are unable to get the best performance out of yourself when you are in a bad mood or when you are too preoccupied with the idea that there is a possibility that you can make a difference. Because you are worried about something, there are moments when you get the impression that you are powerless to take any action at all, even if you really want to. It is not due to the fact that you have previously been unsuccessful in doing these tasks. In point of fact, you may have never even given it a go before. Simply put, you are experiencing a high level of anxiety, to the point that your body is physically responding to the circumstances: your hands are sweating, and you have the sensation that you are about to vomit up.

The majority of the time, negative feelings are the result of terrible experiences that a person has had in the past. These experiences might be so upsetting that a person is conditioned to constantly assume that similar circumstances will always arise again. It is possible for you to assume that at times it is similar to when you were a child and you were attempting to reason with your mother, who would constantly tell you that you are incapable of doing anything correctly. Even though you have been living on your own for some time now, she insisted throughout the course of many years that you would continue to have the sensation that you are battling for your right to engage in an activity that you have always desired. You may believe that your unfavorable feelings are valid, but in reality, they are not. When you really stop to think about it, you are only cohabitating with phantoms that you invite to live inside of your skull.

Put simply, anchoring

Anchoring is a technique that may assist you in overcoming the bad feelings that you are experiencing when you feel as if you are not prepared to perform anything that you are meant to do due to anxiousness. Instead of struggling against emotions that do not make sense, why not try associating a different emotion, preferably a pleasant one, with a circumstance that causes you to feel stressed out?

Anchoring is the process of identifying a feeling with a certain stimulus, which would function as the control within your brain. This is done so that the emotion may be anchored. Your brain would assume that the stimulus and the feeling function well together, and that when the stimulus occurs, the sensation would be felt. This is because your brain believes that they operate well together. In this manner, you will always have the option to employ the stimulus to experience something that has the potential to make you feel better.

For instance, if you usually feel worried whenever you are obliged to speak in front of a group of people, you could believe that the feeling that you MUST have while you are with unknown people is tension because of your past experiences. What if, on the other hand, you could replace the tension with joy, which is how you feel everytime you see your dog become better and better at a skill that you've taught him? This is the procedure for doing that:

1. Visualize your pet appearing on a movie screen and attempting to do some kind of feat, like catching a ball. There is a lever right next to you that is linked to the display screen.

2. Picture the picture you see on the screen coming to life and taking on such vivid color that you begin to question whether or not it is a simulation or the genuine thing. You start to have the sensation that you are becoming thrilled, and you realize that you are feeling excited because you know that the next time you throw the ball, your dog will undoubtedly be able to catch it and deliver it back to you. Perform the motion as though you are holding your dog's favorite chew toy to heighten the intensity of the feeling you are now experiencing.

3. Visualize that you are pulling up on the lever, and that this action takes you closer to the screen, to the point where you nearly have the impression that you are a part of the picture, even if you are still seeing it. 4. Now, imagine that you are pulling up on the lever, and that this action brings you even closer to the screen. You are able to make out every little thing and every hue. You can almost make out the sound of your dog's excited panting as he anticipates the ball that you are holding in your palm. Imagine a voice speaking to you in your thoughts and telling you, "Let the fun begin."

4. After you have finished appreciating the moment, return the lever to the position it was in before. You are able to sense that your body is starting to connect the pleasure that you are feeling with the activity that you are required to do. You will, from this point on, experience the same level of excitement anytime you are required to speak in

front of a big number of people just as you did throughout this exercise.

Another trick that you may do with the use of NLP is shown here. It's possible that you occasionally hear yourself telling yourself that you can't complete a task or that you shouldn't even bother trying to participate in an activity because you don't have what it takes to do so.

Imagine the voice that you hear when you close your eyes and think about it. Is it possible that it may be the voice of someone you know? You would most likely be hearing the taunts of the bully who previously harassed you, as well as those of the cynical instructor or supervisor who always had doubts about you. Now, take that voice and give it the characteristics of someone whose voice you probably won't have the opportunity to hear in person during your lifetime, such as Richard Nixon. You may also give it a voice that is so ridiculous that you can't possibly take anything that it says seriously, like

Donald Duck, for example. This is another option. Now, it does not matter what nasty things you would find yourself saying against you since you would hear them in the least convincing manner possible.

Enhance the Wonderful Sense That You Have

There may be times when you feel as if you need to force yourself to think joyful thoughts in order to be successful in accomplishing a goal. That may be the presentation you are going to give in front of your important employer later, or it could be the marathon that you are about to run. Either way, you have a lot riding on this. You are aware that once you are in a good mood, you have the impression that you cannot be stopped, thus the course of action that you believe you need to take is most certainly the correct one. Here is how you may get a hold of the most upbeat emotions that you can possibly imagine having.

1. Bring your eyes to a close. Think back to the most amazing and satisfying event

you've ever had, the one that left you with the most lasting and powerful impression of happiness you've ever had. Create a mental image of the event and try to recall the feelings that you had throughout it. Look at what you have looked at, and listen to what you have listened to.

2. As the wonderful feeling washes over you, you should attempt to determine where it first begins. Do you feel it in the back of your neck or do you feel it in the tips of your fingers?

3. Eliminate any further consideration of the event. Does the pleasant feeling leave your body straight afterwards, or does it linger in some other part of it?

4. Recall the uplifting event in your mind and concentrate on the feeling that it stirs up inside you. Pull the feeling back from the portion of your body where you initially experienced it just before the sensation goes when your mind wanders to focus about anything else, such as the work at hand. This should happen just before the sensation really leaves.

Continue repeating that until you have the feeling that the sensation is going to keep going around and around your whole body and spinning faster and faster.

5. You would get the notion that the happy feeling is becoming stronger the quicker it loops around your body and the faster it rotates. You may now take pleasure in the feeling even while you engage in another activity.

Now that you are aware that it is possible for you to exert control over your feelings, you also understand that it is not difficult to eliminate the unfavorable emotions that hinder you from seeing your surroundings in the manner in which they really exist. You are also aware that it is possible for you to experience happy emotions yourself and then radiate those feelings toward other people. When you take a closer look, you'll see that this presents an opportunity for you to understand and influence the behavior of others.

An Introduction ToNlp

Neuro-linguistic programming is based on three fundamental tenets of human excellence: having strong convictions and being open to questioning those beliefs, having a well-organized mind and the capacity to think clearly, and being aware of the mind-body link and knowing how to make use of it.

Consider that practicing NLP is similar to going on a mental trip. Put your eyes out of your mind and envision a door. After opening it, you will find yourself in a lengthy hallway. In this initial stage of the trip, you will investigate the beliefs that you currently hold. In what do you put your faith? Who do you value more: yourself, a higher power or religion, your friends and family, or all of the above? During your mental stroll, give some serious consideration to the things that you believe in and the things that you would want to believe in.

Imagine that you are leading your own mind on a trip via NLP.

During this mental stroll, you have the opportunity to evaluate whether or not your current beliefs are sufficient for you, and if they are not, you may consider the most effective means by which to modify them. You'll be able to see a second door when you've traversed the mental corridor and reached a point where you're satisfied with the current status of your beliefs.

After passing through the second door, you will come to a vast area that is crammed with shelves and other things. This chamber is a representation of your brain. How well does it have things organized? Do you keep track of your ideas and emotions in a methodical way, or do you just let everything kind of jumble about in your head? You will be able to assess whether or not it is necessary for you to make adjustments in your life if you take the time to mentally analyze the file system in your own brain and give it some thought.

People who are more organized, both mentally and physically, have a higher chance of achieving their goals and tend to be more effective as leaders and businesses. This section of your mental trip is when you may take some time for yourself to organize your thoughts and emotions if you feel the need to do so. When you are comfortable with the way information is stored in your brain, you may go ahead and open the door to the far side of your mental library.

The chamber that can be found beyond the third door has two different pieces of furniture in it. The first is a majestic throne, while the second is a crude seat that was hand-hewn. Which one would you say you have earned the right to sit on? Try your hand at both of them. You probably like sitting on the throne quite a bit, but ask yourself whether you are really deserving of it. As you are now seated on the stool, how do you feel? It's likely that you have a gloomy mood, as seen by the way your shoulders are hunched and the fact that you seem to be uncomfortable in this posture. You have to have confidence in your own ability to sit on the throne if you ever want to achieve that goal. Maintain an upright posture. Do you feel how amazing that posture makes you feel? You need to walk with an air of confidence, erectness, and loftiness about you.

Savor the sensation of sitting on the throne, but at the same time, don't forget what it was like to sit on the stool. This will serve as a reminder of both where you started and where you ultimately aspire to go. Once you have firmly established in your mind the mental image and sensations of sitting on the throne, your mental trip will be finished. You want to train your mind so that it automatically prompts you to maintain an upright stance and walk with confidence at all times. Many congratulations to you! You have just finished the first session of your basic NLP training. What emotions do you have? Probably a little bit fatigued, but also quite satisfied with what I've accomplished.

Taking the Next Steps in NLP

After you have completed one or two first journeys using NLP, you may start utilizing the mental journey process to begin setting objectives, making changes in your life, and doing a great deal more. Keep in mind that the purpose of neuro-linguistic programming is already conveyed in its name:

neuro: pertaining to the brain

Linguistic refers to the language that we speak.

Programming is the process of directing something (or someone) to carry out a certain activity.

Through the language you use with yourself, you are figuratively and physically reprogramming your brain to think or behave in a specific manner. You might tell yourself that you want to lose weight or stop smoking by visualizing a corridor and many rooms in your house. Continuing with the theme of losing weight, let's assume your goal is to shed twenty pounds.

Open the first door of your mind as yourself, complete with the height and look you have right now. While you are walking down the hallway, give some thought to the reasons you would want to lose weight as well as the circumstances that lead to your dissatisfaction with your current weight. Have you just switched to a less physically demanding work at which you burn fewer calories? Have you lately been through a difficult emotional experience that caused a shift in your eating habits? Before you go through the second door, you need to first determine the circumstances at play as well as your motive for doing so.

When you enter the door, you will find yourself in a room that is stacked to the ceiling with food. All kinds, including those that are good for you and those that are bad for you, sweet and salty, fresh and processed. This area will be filled with a diverse range of individuals, including those who are skinny, overweight, tall, short, healthy, and unhealthy. Take note of the dietary decisions that those other folks are making as well as how they seem to you. Your eating habits should probably be modeled after someone in this room; who would you choose? Open the third door after you have watched everything that is taking place in the previous room, thought about how you want to appear, and decided how you should eat in order to achieve that goal.

In the last chamber, see yourself as you would want to be and how you would like to appear. Create a clear image in your mind. Now that you've made the decision to abstain from unhealthy meals, think of something ridiculous that you might do with them instead. Imagine a cliff with a bottomless pit over which you can toss fried delicacies like french fries. Imagine loading several bags of chips onto a catapult and then firing them far away from you and your life. This makes no sense at all, but you are attempting to leave an imprint in your own head, therefore it doesn't matter if it sounds absurd. Open your eyes and continue going about your day after you have finished purging the thought of junk food from your mind. But everytime you find yourself in a difficult situation, just remember your chip catapult. You'll have a good laugh at yourself, and you won't end up eating any of the chips.

Convincing yourself that the meal you wish to consume has a revolting flavor is yet another strategy you may use to get through the last chamber. Imagine you are eating a hamburger from a fast food restaurant, but the burger is very astringent and unpleasant to eat. When you think of fast food again, you will remember that it doesn't even have a very pleasant flavor to it. This is the impression you will have left yourself with.

You may also use NLP to educate yourself how to have higher self-esteem, improve your study habits, explore your personal beliefs on a deeper level, teach yourself how to teach yourself to have higher self-esteem, or address emotional difficulties. When you've mastered the skill of influencing yourself, you'll be in a much better position to protect yourself from being manipulated by other people. NLP is one of the most valuable tools you can use to do this, and once you've learned it, it's one of the most useful things you can employ. You'll also be better able to manipulate other people and engage in other sorts of dark psychology after you've mastered these skills.

The time spent learning NLP is time well spent since it is such a flexible way of introspection and self-manipulation that it might take a while to become proficient at it. However, the time spent learning it is well worth it. Do not give up on it even if you give it a few tries and find that you are unsuccessful. The more you engage in NLP practice, the more intuitive and simple it will become. When you practice your NLP, it's best to do it in a calm environment where you won't be disturbed too much. You may put on some soft background music for yourself if you prefer, or any other form of ambient sounds that will assist you in unwinding and calming down. If you're feeling uneasy or stressed out, there's a strong possibility that your NLP session won't be nearly as successful as it might be. One of the secrets to practicing excellent NLP is to let your mind wander while yet being hyper-focused, and if you do this, you'll be able to practice it better.

You will eventually become so great at NLP that even when you need to give yourself a little pep talk, you will be able to shut your eyes and race around your mental corridors to give yourself a fast refresher or mental pick-me-up. Eventually, you will become so skilled at NLP that you will be able to do this even when you need to give yourself a little pep talk. You may also use this method to swiftly validate or reevaluate a notion or opinion that you have. You may use NLP whenever you need to work through a problem or a challenging scenario since it is a practice that you can apply at any moment. You could even become so knowledgeable that you are able to instruct other people or lead them on a mentally guided trip towards achieving their objectives. Or it might be yours; just keep in mind that the mental power is in your control.

To further discuss Journeys...

Our adventure into the realm of dark psychology has come to an end with this conversation on neuro-linguistic programming and training your brain to take a mental journey. We hope you enjoyed our time spent together exploring this fascinating field. This book should serve as a guide for you on your journey to understanding how dark psychology may operate for you and against you, as well as how to deal with dark psychology if and when it presents itself to you. The knowledge that you have acquired in this book should serve as a guide for you. Always remember to trust your instincts, even after all other options have been exhausted, and to take an active role in observing and engaging with the environment around you. The only way we can genuinely understand how to exert influence over humans is by getting to know them and engaging with them.

Using NLP To Erase Unpleasant Memories

There are both positive and negative experiences to be had during one's lifetime. Every one of these recollections is stored in a device that we refer to as "memory." Your memory stores both the good and the terrible events you've had, and although the former may be a source of happiness when you think back on them, the latter can be a source of anxiety.

The use of NLP may help you get insight into how you can effectively manage your negative memories and replace them with positive ones. In addition to this, the Neuro-Linguistic Programming (NLP) training will show you how to retrieve painful memories from your subconscious without being overcome with negative feelings. In turn, this will help you to see the traumatic experience from the past in a detached manner and learn from the experience as a result.

It's not the terrible memories themselves that are the problem; it's how you choose to think about them that has a significant impact on who you are. When you focus on the negative aspects of memories, you give those memories more strength and the opportunity to return to you as ghosts. The reason why your negative memories are able to "get the best of you" is because you tend to recollect them in a manner that is related with other memories. When you think back on a negative event, you automatically connect it with the emotional baggage that you carried away from it. If you pay careful attention, you may notice that these feelings are not all that unlike to those you had in the past.

Quit your habit

One of the most unhealthybehaviors is smoking cigarettes. Not only is it terrible for you and everyone else in the immediate area, but it also makes you smell terrible. This is a double whammy. Additionally, it hastens the aging process. It may come as a surprise to you to find that Neuro-Linguistic Programming may also assist you in breaking this undesirable pattern of behavior.

When it comes to quitting smoking, neuro-linguistic programming (NLP) and hypnosis are often utilized in combination with one another as complementary treatment modalities. Your chance of being successful is much increased when you make use of both of these components, as opposed to when you just use one of these strategies.

Establishing a negative anchor that you link with smoking should be the first step in quitting smoking. This may be done with or without the use of hypnosis. It might be a series of ideas, similar to what we mentioned before with regards to meals and activities, or it could be something you touch to remind you that smoking is a negative habit that you want to get rid of.

Using NLP to Efficiently Reduce Your Levels of Stress

Because stress plays such a significant role in the lives of people living in the present day, it is important to investigate how neuro-linguistic programming (NLP) may successfully assist you in lowering the amount of stress in your life, if not entirely removing it.

No matter how much you manage to better yourself and how great you become at anything, there will always be a certain degree of tension in your life. It is impossible to avoid stress entirely. This is a truth that must be faced by each and every one of us. If you wish to live in today's contemporary civilization, there is no such thing as a stress-free atmosphere, since there is no such thing.

The trouble is that stress may cause your brain to produce some pretty dangerous chemicals, and the damage caused by those chemicals can have repercussions that last a long time. Your performance and the clarity of your thinking are both going to decrease when you are under a significant amount of stress. Even while it is impossible to totally prevent stress, there are many things that can be done to lessen the bad affects that it has on both the body and the mind.

The Art of Questioning to Influence Others

When it comes to convincing someone of anything, asking thoughtful questions may be really effective. The following is a list of the actions that you need to do in order to ask compelling questions in order to convince someone:

In the first step of this process, you will choose the primary premises upon which your argument will be based. For instance, if you wish to argue for receiving two days off from work, you should first investigate the reasons behind your desire for the time off and ensure that your assumptions are accurate.

The second step is to test your hypotheses by asking questions. For instance, if your justification for requesting two days off from work was that "I will be able to work more productively after the time off," you might reframe your justification as a question by asking, "Don't you think that I'll be able to work more productively after the time off?"

Step 3: Tailor your assumption to your topic by using the information provided. For instance, if your topic is your supervisor, you need to convince him that your assumptions are correct. Because he doesn't care about productivity, there's no use in trying to convince him of anything. To put it another way, your assumption should be something that is important to the person you are studying. An emotionally charged assumption is effective when applied to those who are emotional.

Step 4: Schedule regular time in your schedule to engage in practice. It takes more time to formulate compelling questions than it does to formulate persuasive responses.

The fifth step is to either write down your questions or give them some serious consideration before you ask them.

Enjoy the effect that your inquiries have on other people, which is the sixth step.

Where You Ought To Make Use Of Nlp

There are various applications for NLP in a variety of spheres of life. In the next section, we will discuss the many settings in which you may put the principles of NLP into practice.

Conversations about one's private life

Maintaining open lines of communication with one another is of the utmost significance. You won't have to bottle up your emotions since it will show you how to appropriately express them and free you from the obligation to do so. You will also be able to avoid getting into conflicts at home that aren't essential, which will give you more peace of mind. Additionally, communication will assist you in leading a more fulfilling life and will bring you and your family closer together. our is of utmost significance in our day and age, when most individuals fail to see the significance of cultivating and sustaining meaningful connections with others.

Consider your own worth.

You will learn how to appreciate yourself using NLP. As you are aware, how you see things has a significant role in how you react to the world around you, and it is common knowledge that individuals tend to be too critical of themselves. However, in order to achieve success, you need to first love who you are. You have to admit that your mental process is valid and then assess it. Don't be too hard on yourself for the bad qualities; you have the ability to work on them and improve them. You have to play the hero by focusing on your good qualities and pursuing them.

Alterations for the better

The use of NLP will result in a significant improvement. You and the members of your family will be successful in achieving your objectives and living a satisfying life. The development of excellent connections can assist you in warding off unneeded stress and difficulties in your life. Building a strong connection with one another will go a long way toward assisting you in achieving greater levels of self-confidence. You will never have to worry about whether or not you will have the support of your family because you will be able to rest certain that they will be there for you no matter what challenges you face in life.

a life in the working world

Implementing NLP is a strategy that may bring you a great deal of success in your professional life.

The resolution of issues

Problem solving at work is one of the most crucial duties, and if you step up to the challenge and shine, then there is no doubt that others will take note of you. You might make a good impression on your manager, which could lead to a pay raise. But before you can do that, you need to get familiar with NLP and know how to efficiently solve issues. You are aware that communication is of the utmost significance, and as a result, prior to settling upon a solution, you will be required to speak with your colleagues and co-workers and to pay attention to all of their input.

In charge

You will have an easier time managing the many individuals that work in your workplace if you are trained in NLP. When there are a lot of people working in your office and it is your obligation to make sure they are all on the same page, people management may seem like a burdensome chore at times. However, it is particularly crucial when there are a lot of people working in your office. You'll learn patience and how to take the initiative with NLP training. It will not be difficult at all for you to convince everyone to pay attention to what it is that you have to say. Once again, your managerial abilities might be the key to your success in climbing the corporate ladder.

Administration of Power

Leadership abilities are essential, particularly if you want to contribute to the development of your firm. guiding adults is a far more difficult task than guiding toddlers. It is necessary for you to keep everyone pleased and pay attention to what each person has to say. Both patience and the skill to maintain order in a large gathering are essential. You will be able to do everything with relative ease if you put certain NLP techniques into practice. As was said previously, successful individuals are aware of the appropriate moments to take action and make the most of their capabilities. Because of this, the leader will be able to become even more powerful.

Amounts Sold

Increasing sales is a goal that should be a priority for every business, but doing it successfully may be challenging. You have to put in the effort to identify the most lucrative items or services in order to draw in the most customers. Improving how well you communicate with your team will help you achieve higher sales statistics. In order to maintain a winning streak, you need to make it a priority to research the past of your firm, determine what strategies were successful, and then use those strategies going forward.

Assistance to customers

It's possible that a company's customers are the most significant part of the business. If you want to be successful in business, you have to make sure that your clients are satisfied. In order to accomplish this goal, you will need to develop open lines of contact with them. As you already know, NLP may assist you in speaking freely and clearly, allowing you to more effectively communicate with your audience. You will be able to find solutions to their problems in a more timely manner, which will make them pleased.

It is important to keep in mind that the benefits of using NLP in your work life are not confined to the aforementioned categories; the list may go on and on.

You will get familiar with the additional advantages of NLP as you use it and as you do so in the future.

Taking Care of Objections

It is my sincere hope that you will be able to execute the five-step procedure to such a high standard that you will never face any opposition to your conclusion. However, there are going to be moments when you just are not going to do it right the very first time. How should one respond when faced with the dreaded objection?

The first tactic is to disregard the opposition.

The fact that you did not provide sufficient value in step 3 is the foundation for any objections that may be raised. My initial plan of action is to disregard the criticism and concentrate instead on enhancing the value of what I provide.

The second tactic is to deal with the obstacle.

Again, if you've built up enough value, nobody will have a problem with what you're offering. If you give someone who is about to die of thirst something to drink and they accept your offer, they will pay whatever price you want for that water. A fast search on Google for "handling objections" can provide you with some helpful hints and suggestions. I've included a few of mine down below for your perusal.

The act of responding to a counterargument is known as "reframing." Your task is to reframe the issue such that it seems to be something that isn't a problem at all. As I've said in the past, the "What if..." frame is the one that I find myself turning to the majority of the time. It seems that either time or money is the source of virtually all of the concerns. Therefore, one of my favorite questions to ask is, "Supposing you had sufficient amounts of time and money, where would you get them?" This rapidly dispels any notion held by the prospect that they are unable to afford or devote the necessary amount of time to the venture. The vast majority of the time, they will admit that they could get the money; nevertheless, they had never considered doing it in that manner. It's incredible how that can happen!

The following is yet another solid option in terms of cost: Put the cost of the item or service that you are selling down on paper. The next step is to inquire with the potential customer about the price range that they are comfortable with paying. Now take his ability to pay and deduct the amount you're asking from that number. If you want to sell them on the difference, you should cross out the previous numbers and/or circle the new figure.

For illustration purposes, the fee for my lecture is $1997. I inquire about the potential customer's budget for the event. The potential customer claims to have $1500 available.

I calculate that $1997 minus $1500 is $497.

After that, I strike through the first two.

In addition, circle the final number.

Then I respond with, "So you're telling me that you don't have $497. That won't be an issue at all since we provide flexible payment options. You are able to make the payment over the course of the following several months." I am simply focusing on the $497 portion of the problem rather than attempting to find a solution to the complete $1997 amount. When working with a lesser quantity, a prospect will almost always have an easier time. The fewer the numbers, the more they resemble the more manageable challenges. When dealing with objections, it is important to strive to reduce the amount of them as much as you can.

The last objection closure is the final strategy that I employ to address objections. It's a simple reframing that can be explained as follows:

Pay careful attention to the prospect's counterargument.

Pretend to be a little bit taken aback.

Say something like, "Oh, I see. Do you really mean to claim that's the sole reason you won't be buying?"

Say something along the lines of, "If I could show you how to have (whatever the objection is), then would you buy it?"

Then you should immediately return to determining the worth of anything.

My research has shown that the majority of individuals only have four key criticisms to offer:

1. "I'm sorry, but I don't have enough time."

2. "I don't have enough money," the speaker said.

3. "It isn't going to work for me, but it might for other people."

4. "It won't work for me (it doesn't work for anyone)," the person said.

The correct response to each of these objections is "That's why you need my product or service." Obviously supposing that your company's product or service offers a solution to these issues.

Testimonials are the solution to objections number three and four. Share examples of previous customers who had the same beliefs as you but have now come to a different conclusion. I actually have previous customers that I can contact and ask if they would be willing to provide a testimonial over the phone for my prospects. That is the power that comes from having rapport.

It Is Completely Dependent Upon Your Conduct.

What factors contribute to our behaviors? Where do they get their supplies? When we look back on a situation, many of us find ourselves wishing that we had performed differently: that we had kept our calm, been less worried, been more extroverted, not thrown that first punch, acted more politely, and been less aggressive. The question is, therefore, what influences our behavior. Is it possible to separate it and comprehend it? Without a doubt! NLP may be used to break into the thinking patterns that lead to behavior, which is one of the most significant advantages of using NLP. Our actions may be characterized by extremes of optimism or pessimism, aggressiveness or passivity, assertiveness or passivity, trust or envy, or any combination of these. The way we behave is so often the product of many deeper layers of information in our brains; things that we maybe aren't even aware of since they are such unconscious ideas and attitudes.

The strategies that are detailed in this book will teach you how to get to the bottom of how your actions shape your life and where those habits originated from. You will also get an understanding of how to modify your behavior. One scenario in which this may apply is if you have been trying to lose weight for some time and have tried various diets and exercise routines, but nothing seems to work. Your conduct is passive due to the fact that you are not establishing your will to achieve your objectives, and it is also jealous due to the fact that you are assuming that you need to lose weight in order to measure up to other people's standard of beauty. You may even exhibit gloomy conduct as a result of the fact that you have given up after making several efforts that were unsuccessful.

You will be able to discover HOW to modify these habits after NLP has assisted you in identifying the underlying thinking patterns that are the root of the problem. A significant portion of psychotherapy is dedicated to illuminating ingrained behavior patterns by investigating the reasons that underlie such patterns. NLP places a greater emphasis on the how.

The dark triad is a psychological model of individual characteristics that consists of three personality traits: narcissism, psychopathy, and Machiavellianism. This model was developed by psychologists. A feeling of self-exclusivity, a need to be the center of attention, and an attitude that is dismissive of other people are all hallmarks of narcissism. A guy who suffers from narcissistic personality disorder really believes that he is better than other people and is convinced that his goals and aspirations should come before those of others. A lack of emotional sensitivity, a lack of self-control, a need for thrills, an absence of fear, and a feeling of one's superiority are all characteristics of a person who suffers from psychopathy. A person with psychopathy is by nature defiant and independent. A high score on the Machiavellian scale indicates that a person has a low degree of empathy, a predisposition for manipulation, and immorality. These are the characteristics that define a Machiavellian.

Sincerely adheres to the principle that "the means justify the end." Machiavellianism is distinguished from narcissism and psychopathy not by the inherent characteristics of the individual, but rather by the manner in which they manipulate other people. A guy with Machiavellianism would, in contrast to narcissists and psychopaths, actively manipulate others; for him, other people are nothing more than a means to an end in order to accomplish his objectives.

It was first narcissism, then psychopathy, and finally Machiavellianism that were brought to the attention of humankind. First and foremost, psychoanalysts began discussing narcissism for the very first time. Since the beginning of the 19th century, people have been describing characteristics of the personality that are connected with having an inflated sense of self-importance. And this sensation did not make the narcissists themselves happy; instead, individuals suffered from self-criticism and loneliness, and they found it difficult to establish and sustain connections with other people. It might be challenging to maintain a meaningful connection with a person who has the firm conviction that the center of the universe ought to be occupied by him alone. Narcissus is not capable of seeing the wants of others, is not willing to compromise, and has an extremely abrasive response to criticism. And it is not easy either to be such a person or to be with someone who fits this description.

Around the turn of the 21st century, people started talking about non-clinical narcissism for the first time. 1979 saw the development of one of the very first surveys specifically designed to discover narcissistic characteristics in individuals who were otherwise considered to be typical. These days, there are already a number of different surveys. Researchers feel that narcissism is a combination of qualities, not a "root" personality trait, with its varied expressions; yet, there is no test that can accurately diagnose narcissism.

During the course of the research conducted on convicts, psychopathy was uncovered. Psychologists who were researching criminals around the end of the 19th century began to speculate about the factors that led to antisocial conduct. They were under the impression that there was a justification for their breaching the law. In the beginning of the study, the researchers had experts explain characteristics that are typical of criminals. These included a lack of fear, a low level of anxiety, a tendency toward antisocial conduct, egocentrism, a lack of empathy and empathy for others, impulsivity, and a poor degree of self-control. These characteristics served as the foundation for a particular version of the sociopath personality disorder, which doctors then started diagnosing.

For instance, one of the researchers of psychopathic psychology professor Robert Haer in his study, which subsequently became the book "The Frightening World of Psychopaths," demonstrated that the jail system that is now in place in the United States is ineffective for persons who have a high degree of psychopathy. Psychopaths, rather than reforming, acted contrite and obedient, which ultimately led to their release from captivity. On the other hand, they were eventually sent back to jail for additional charges, which was something that occurred to them more often than it did to persons who did not have psychopathic tendencies.

These days, psychopathic tendencies may be found in individuals and are considered to be the norm, particularly in persons who have not engaged in any unlawful behavior. Psychopathy, both primary and secondary, is a topic that is constantly debated in the scientific community. There is a strong correlation between specific hereditary characteristics and primary psychopathy. A total or partial lack of empathy, for instance, might be brought on by circumstances related to genetics. This mechanism has historically been considered a fundamental one for humans and has played an extremely essential role in the development of our species. It's not like there's a DNA for empathy or anything like that. The fundamental psychopathy may be responsible for biological elements, such as those linked with the formation of mirror neurons, which are responsible for the bodily manifestations of empathy, according to the research conducted by scientists.

Secondary psychopathy is a kind of psychopathy that develops in people as a personality characteristic as a result of bad developmental settings. They result in a loss of self-control, the maturation of impulsivity, and other repercussions that pave the way for antisocial conduct. Psychologists, on the other hand, are more concerned with the severity of the disorder's characteristics and how they manifest themselves in many aspects of a patient's life rather than its underlying nature.

The machiavellian theory was first put to the test in the 1970s. The so-called Mc Scale was conceived by and created by Richard Christie and Florence Gays. It is possible to utilize it to evaluate a person's inclination to influence other individuals within the context of interpersonal interactions. This test reveals a person's general lack of faith in the ability of others to be relied upon. Researchers of the modern day investigate several aspects of Machiavellianism; nevertheless, they do not yet play a significant part in the process of preventing manipulative conduct.

Research on narcissism, psychopathy, and Machiavellianism were conducted independently up to the turn of the 20th and 21st century. Nevertheless, very lately, these characteristics have been categorized as qualities that are typical of the shadowy, unfavorable aspect of the personality. Since the beginning of the 21st century, researchers have been attempting to ascertain whether or not these three characteristics are distinct from one another or just represent diverse expressions of the same traditional dark core of the human being.

Researchers in the modern day feel that all of these characteristics have a fundamental component; nevertheless, they also acknowledge that each has its own unique qualities. Therefore, in today's world, the extroversion, kindness, conscientiousness, neuroticism, and openness to new experiences facets of a person's personality are regarded to constitute the "Big Five," while the "dark triad" is believed to be an addition to this traditional personality model.

And if the big five are characteristics that are generally accepted in society, the dark triad consists of characteristics of one's personality that contribute to maladaptation.

NLP Fundamentals

According to the neuro-linguistic programming (NLP), human habits have been shaped by behavioral patterns and habits. If a person is aware of their routines, patterns, and behavior, it will be feasible for them to understand how to exercise control over their own life. The field of study known as NLP covers a vast and varied subject matter; nevertheless, in a nutshell, it examines what drives us and the factors that influence the choices we make. They are also known as metaprograms in the industry.

What exactly are these "Metaprograms"? The mental process is what directs, controls, and ultimately decides on the many mental challenges that arise. In addition, it decides on the outcomes of other intellectually taxing procedures. The phrase originates from a word used in the field of computer science. In addition, it is a reference to the practicality of the software applications. When the phrase is disassembled into its component parts, meta, which means anything on a higher level, and programs, which means the instructions that let a computer or PC work, are all that it refers to.

Metaprograms are the major and main programs that are recognized as built-in behaviors. They are also known as "primary" programs. Additionally, they are in charge of directing other programs on the computer, which is essentially your mind. There are a great deal of metaprograms available in the field of NLP. There are five that are described below, each of which may appear in a slightly different form when used on the internet.

There are two different versions of metaprograms, and no one person completely fits into either one. And there are certain persons who fit the bill for each of these interpretations. This is due to the fact that they define the reasons why individuals behave the way they do, as well as how they might be categorized into different categories. In addition, they are not intended to differentiate between the characteristics and actions of individuals. The most prevalent types of metaprograms will determine how the mind works, how the mind operates, and how it will judge the behavior that is involved.

The sameness and the diversity are both included in it.

The sameness version is the one that is constantly inspired by similar things, they are aware of similarities, and they always search for activities that are inside their comfort zone. They gain confidence in what they desire because of the feeling of familiarity, and they end up enjoying the things they are seeking for as a result. In addition to this, every circumstance from one's previous experiences. And they benefit positively from having it repeated to them.

On the other hand, there is always going to be a difference between items when looking at different versions. They like change and are constantly eager to learn new things, and they are not afraid to experiment with diverse activities. They hunt for things that are inconsistent, and if they find them, they alter them very immediately. They are always looking for ways to improve things, despite the fact that there is no need for them to do so. They are aware of and grasp the possibilities because they are aware of and comprehend the disparities.

Away from something while moving toward it

To put it another way, the concept that these individuals on the towards qualities would eventually succeed in what they set out to do is the primary force that drives them. They get their happiness and fulfillment from the successful completion of their goals. Having to create objectives, which can be done quickly and regularly, is what drives people to get things done. They are driven to finish everything on their to-do list by their ambition and desire to succeed. And ultimately provides them with the sensation that they have been gratified.

The other interpretations imply that they are solely concerned with avoiding the potential for suffering or danger that may be experienced. The capacity to escape from difficult situations is what keeps them going. They have the impression that they are secure and well provided for. Before doing anything, they have ensured that they are clear of any challenges and problems.

Both the outside and the inside

Those who work on the inside are the ones who decide what the standards are. They establish criteria that allow them to feel at ease with the approval process and with selecting choices. They don't bother looking for any kind of proof that they did a good job or that they are making the best choice possible. They always know when they have done something correctly and think that they have attained the objectives and standards that they have set for themselves. When presented with an excessive amount of information, it has a demotivating effect on them, and they always want space to achieve their objectives.

Those that are shown on the exterior version and are reliant on the permission, guidance, and standards of other individuals. They like having someone oversee and monitor them, as well as having someone congratulate them on their accomplishments on a regular basis. They get the sense that they are understood, valued, and approved of as a result of this gesture. They always have poor motivation and are unsure of their skills when they don't receive any feedback, thus it's important to provide it to them.

The process that is involved as well as the available choices

When they have a comprehensive understanding of everything and everything, they always search for the alternative that is ideal for them among those available. They are not concerned with the minute particulars and would rather have more options. They have the choice to learn more about who they are and what they are capable of.

Those individuals who are actively participating in the process put in a lot of effort whenever they are asked questions that need a response. They make sure that everything is handled in the appropriate manner at all times and coordinate all of the necessary data. They constantly wish that they were provided all the knowledge, such as following procedures and frameworks, since they find that this helps them perform more effectively.

Both of these are examples of reactive and proactive action.

In the proactive approach, these individuals are referred regarded as initiators. They never go behind schedule and always do their work in a timely manner. They are only concerned with what is happening right now and do not give any thought to what could occur in the future. They never lose sight of what is really taking place and maintain the attitude that everything is tangible and ought to be genuine. They never lose focus on the tasks at hand, whether those chores have already been completed or remain unfinished.

The reactive type is the kind of person that constantly spends a lot of time preparing and evaluating everything in their environment. Each and every one of their choices is required to go through a well designed process. They construct their own timetable and schedule their activities accordingly in order to keep track of their progress. They are always concerned with what they should schedule and access. And constantly keeping a watchful eye out for the optimal moment to plan and carry out a job.

There are situations in which the majority of individuals will have a combination of different patterns and versions. And yet some have a stronger preference for one camp than the other.

In spite of everything, NLP metaprograms are a fascinating component since they travel into the human mind and provide people the ability to comprehend themselves. People are able to better comprehend one another as a result of the variances, which in turn leads to improved productivity. They always have a good awareness of the personal preferences and routines of other individuals. In addition, it establishes more connections. NLP enables one to get complete control of one's mind and also recognizes how the mind operates; this enables the mind to perform more effectively and constantly assists in the development of a more optimistic mindset. Put up maximum effort in their respective jobs.

Exercise No. 1 in Relationships

Find someone you do not know very well and strike up a conversation with them while mimicking their posture and the way their body moves. In order to avoid being caught, you need make sure that you wait five seconds after they have moved before you step into their body posture and area.

Exercise No. 2 on Relationships

Carry out the activity described above, but this time make the assumption that you already have a connection with the other person. It implies starting with the assumption that you like the other person, that you have known them for a long time, and that you are able to get along with one another in a natural way.

By completing these activities, you will not only develop an appreciation for the power of reporting but also, ideally, an appreciation for the difficulty of mind management. There is also the possibility that you may start seeing people as unique persons rather than as things that can be managed. This last remark is in reality a benefit for you since it will help you lay a velvet glove over the iron fist of power that you are seeking to wield due of the fact that you want to control their thoughts.

Maintaining and taking the lead

In any event, pacing and leading are two elements that may be used in a variety of ways.

First, the leader must pace, which indicates that he or she imitates the actions of the follower in some way, and then they must lead by doing an action that establishes themselves as the authority figure and compels the follower to comply.

As was mentioned before, the use of pacing and leading is an essential component of the traditional reporting activities. In this context, the controller will organize the subject's movement according to a plan.

In almost every circumstance, taking the lead may also be accomplished via the use of pacing and direction.

Linguistically speaking, pacing and leading take the shape of something called a speed, which is something that is true and can be verified by the subject, and a lead, which is a statement that the controller wants the subject to agree with. This kind of pacing and leading often adheres to the tried-and-true formula of drive, drive, pace, and lead.

Anything like that might sound like: "We're here (pace), you're sitting here (pace) and we're talking (pace) and there's something interesting happening that you may not be aware of (lead), time is moving (pace), it's always happening (pace), we're missing what's really important (lead), but we're here (pace) and when you're concentrating on what's important (lead) you can offer it power and see it (lead) a. It requires a great sensory acuity as well as the capacity to push the subject to follow your direction far sooner than what would typically be the case with pacing and leading.

The operator is given the ability to do a wide variety of tasks because of pacing and leading.

Take note

When someone has concentration, they are completely concentrating on the problem in hand and are choosing to dismiss all of their other concerns, regardless of what those concerns may be.

When you are with your subject as the controller, this implies that all other concerns, such as bills, house payments, and marital arguments, are entirely ignored.

Issues of worry

Concern in the context of a controller is elevating the status of the subject to the same level of significance as the relationship you have with the person you consider to be the most important in your life. Only with the application of your attention and the emotion of love can it be accomplished, even if you have to pretend to feel it.

Affection and firmness of purpose Love and conviction are two sides of the same coin: the belief that what you are doing is right. There are hardly any things that are more important than having complete faith in what it is you do.

Think on the many positive aspects of what you do that are related to the topic at hand in order to inject some life into this concept. These benefits include explanations of why it is required, as well as the ideals, or other things, that it provides you. Also included are these advantages.

By combining certain traits, pacing and leading may be made more straightforward. Both the focus and the worry will help to strengthen the sensory acuity, which may then be utilized to determine whether or not the individual is resisting being led or dragged in any manner. When it detects resistance, the controller will immediately make adjustments to the layout it's using.

The "Function of Physiology" in terms of Neurolinguistic Programming The term "physiology" refers to the way in which the body is utilized to construct and direct mental and emotional experiences. The exposure to such emotional states may be made considerably simpler by making modifications in one's physiology.

Maintaining a mood of despair while engaging in sexual activity is exceedingly challenging for most people.

On the other side, one seems to discover that one might feel despair by slouching over, gazing downward, and having extremely rapid and short breaths. This is one of the classic signs of depression. The fact that so few individuals have really used this strategy is astonishing.

However, it does a fantastic job of controlling the mind. Remember that the ceilings in cathedrals are sometimes quite high and elaborately ornamented. People are compelled to gaze up and reflect how much simpler it is to achieve favorable emotional states as a result of this.

Manipulation in the Place of Employment

At some time in their careers, a significant number of workers will experience some kind of manipulation on the job. Sometimes it is because one of their coworkers is a manipulator, and other times it is due of ordinary kinds of manipulation. Sometimes it is because one of their coworkers is a manipulator. For instance, a coworker may use manipulation to coerce you into assisting them with their assignment or into doing their task for them. They only act in this manner because they despise having to take on this particular task.

There will be moments when you will become aware that your superior is a manipulator. Unfortunately, this is something that occurs much too often in the workplace due to the fact that many bosses have resorted to manipulation in order to achieve their current position, particularly if they made their way up the ladder on their own. However, you should never make the assumption that your boss is trying to manipulate you. If they are, they will generally show indications of being a manipulator, such as bullying, blaming others, making their employees appear guilty, giving their staff the quiet treatment, and manipulating facts. If they are, they will also typically reveal characteristics of being a manipulator.

The manner in which you are dealt with might be used as an indicator that you are collaborating with a manipulator. The manipulators need to ensure that you are aware of your station, which is below them in the hierarchy. As a result, they will often use caustic language to make you feel lower in status than you really are. Take, for instance, the scenario in which you go to work one day dressed in business clothing that is noticeably more laid-back than what is customary at your firm. You make the conscious decision to forego the traditional white shirt and suit in favor of a white shirt paired with pants. Your coworker makes fun of your poor money and the fact that you can't buy finer clothing because of it when they observe your wardrobe and begin to criticize your clothes. They say things like "your clothes are a reflection of your low income."

Techniques For Manipulating Someone's Emotions

Lying is one of the very first strategies that people who manipulate utilize in their arsenal. When they wish to throw their victims for a loop, those who have a pathological need to lie or psychopaths will utilize this tactic. If they repeatedly deceive their victims, the latter are far more likely to be oblivious to the reality of the situation. Those who engage in this strategy do not have any ethical or moral qualms about what they are doing. One further strategy that may be used to influence another person is to just give them part of the tale or to tell them only half of the truth. People with attitudes like these are likely to keep things to themselves because they believe doing so puts the victim in a worse position. They will be able to acquire what they want if they wait to hear the remainder of the narrative until after their requirements have been satisfied.

Being in the company of someone who has frequent shifts in mood may often make a person more susceptible to the manipulations of that person. It may be a highly beneficial strategy for the manipulator to not know what mood the person they are trying to influence will be in, such as whether they will be joyful, sad, or furious. It puts the victim off balance and makes them easier to control because in order to keep them in a good mood, the victim will often do what the manipulator wants them to do.

Love bombing is another strategy that narcissists often use in their interactions with others. This does not imply that you are required to be in a romantic partnership, since it may also be used in the context of a platonic friendship. Those that use this strategy will end up beguiling the victim to the point of death and convincing them that this is the most wonderful romantic or platonic friendship that they have ever had. They will take advantage of the victim to get what they want, and when they are through with them, they will cast them aside so that the victim is unaware of what took place.

The strategy of punishment is one that the manipulator may use in severe circumstances if the need arises. This causes the victim to feel guilty for whatever they did wrong, even if they didn't do anything at all, even if they didn't do anything at all. They are able to subject their victims to a variety of punishments, including persistent nagging, yelling, emotional abuse, the silent treatment, and even something as severe as physical assault.

When a manipulator feels that they are being forced into a corner and they are afraid that they will be shown for the phony that they are, denial is a common strategy that they will utilize. In this scenario, the manipulator will try to trick the victim into thinking that they are engaging in the same behavior that they are accusing the manipulator of engaging in.

Politicians often use the strategy of putting a spin on the truth. It is used to distort the facts so that they fit their requirements or desires better. This tactic is used by sociopaths so that they may conceal their harmful actions and rationalize them in the eyes of their victims.

When a manipulator minimizes their behavior and/or actions, they are playing down their own behavior and/or actions. They shift the responsibility onto the victim for overreacting when their acts are hurtful, and the individual has a genuine basis for feeling the way they do. They do this by shifting the blame onto the victim for overreacting.

When the person who is manipulating claims to be the victim, it may sometimes be amusing to watch. They do this in the hopes that the people they have wronged would feel pity or compassion for them. They do this so that their victims would feel a feeling of obligation to assist them and put an end to their pain, which is particularly important for those victims who believe that they are the cause of the agony of the other person.

Targeting the victim and making false accusations against them is another strategy that the manipulator might use to shift the responsibility onto the victim for their own actions. The victim will then begin to defend themselves, all the while the manipulator will continue to keep the victim unaware of their manipulation. This might be risky since the victim will be so preoccupied with protecting oneself that they won't be paying attention to what is happening in their immediate environment.

By using the strategy of positive reinforcement, the manipulator may fool the victim into believing that they are gaining something in return for their assistance in achieving the manipulator's goals. This may be accomplished in a variety of ways, including buttereding them up, buying them costly things, complimenting them, giving them money, continually apologizing for their actions, giving them a lot of attention, and giving them a lot of attention in general.

There are occasions when a person is aware of the situation they are in with another individual. However, the manipulator may continually shifting the aim in any kind of connection only to confuse their victim, who may have believed that everyone was still on the same page.

Diversion is yet another method of manipulation that those who manipulate others will often use. This strategy is often used by manipulators so that the focus of a particular discourse is taken off of what they are doing. The new subject is introduced with the intention of diverting the victim's attention away from the manipulator's actions or attempts to manipulate them.

By making the target feel embarrassed, sarcasm is a strategy that may be used to bring down the victim's self-esteem and undermine their confidence. In the presence of other people, the manipulator will utilize sarcasm, often by stating something negative about the victim. since of this, the manipulator gains influence over the victim since they have just succeeded in making the victim feel extremely insignificant.

An other strategy that a manipulator will use against their victim is the use of guilt trips. In this situation, they will often tell their victims that they do not love them or care about them; they will also suggest that they are selfish and that their life is simple. It makes the victim confused and nervous because they want to satisfy the manipulator by showing them that they care about them and would do anything for them. This puts the manipulator in control of the situation.

The use of flattery is the antithesis of the technique of guilt-tripping. In this scenario, the manipulator will try to win the victim's confidence by being charming, offering praise, or engaging in other forms of flattery. The target feels flattered by the praises and relaxes their defenses as a result.

When a victim accuses them of using manipulative strategies, a manipulator may try to shift the responsibility by playing the innocent card in an effort to clear their name. They will act as if they are surprised or bewildered by the claim. The victim is convinced, and it causes them to doubt their judgment as well as whether or not what they are experiencing is accurate. This is accomplished by seeming astonished.

Extreme hostility is a risky strategy that a manipulator might utilize if they want to get their way. The victim is subjected to anger and aggressive behavior in order to coerce them into submission. The victim is meant to be intimidated by the angry and furious expressions so that they would stop talking about the dialogue. They seek to assist the manipulator keep his or her rage under control as much as possible.

Another risky strategy that manipulators use is isolating their victims. It is a control technique that is employed by manipulators to keep their victims from their family, friends, and loved ones who are in a position to reveal the manipulator for who they truly are. The manipulator may be aware that their victim can be controlled, but the manipulator's friends and family may see straight through them, and the manipulator is not yet through manipulating their victim.

And last, one of the last strategies that people who are manipulative, like psychopaths and sociopaths, employ is to simulate affection and empathy for their victims. People who are like this are incapable of loving anybody or anything save themselves, and they have a difficult time loving others and demonstrating empathy for other people. They use this strategy to ingratiate themselves into the lives of their victims in order to coerce the victims into giving them what they desire (Learning Mind, 2012).

It is important to keep in mind that Dark Manipulation is a very risky endeavor, and no one should put himself in harm's way by becoming involved with it if they can help it. As a result, it is essential that you read this chapter so that you can guard yourself against anybody who could attempt to take advantage of you and manipulate you in order to acquire what they want. If you are well-informed about these sneaky practices, then it will be much simpler for you to defend yourself against them.

organizations involved with NLP

The absence of a universally accepted standard for regulating the **NLP** certification industry is the source of the issue. In order to do this, peer organizations need to exist and maintain their status. There are a number of organizations that have claimed or presently claim to govern the subject, some of which include the International Association of NLP, the American Board of NLP, the Association for Neuro-Linguistic Programming, and the International Association of NLP-Institutes. It is important to keep in mind that these organizations monitor and ensure that practitioners conform to predetermined criteria, the majority of which are derived from theory that is many decades old. This should not come as a surprise given that almost all credible professional and trade organizations have the same challenge with regard to this issue. Their efforts to maintain the integrity of their doctrine have the unintended consequence of guaranteeing mediocrity and falling behind the times.

Are they using outdated technology?

At some point, every area and discipline will cease to be important. This is also true for ANNH, in addition to NLP. An method that is still coherent with most of what has been disclosed within the fields of neurology, artificial intelligence, and quantum physics – which, coincidentally, are the three pillars that support ANNH – is included inside the **NLP** Communication Model, which serves as the basis of the discipline. Many of the fundamental ideas of NLP, such as the **NLP** Communication Model, are evergreen. It is important to put an emphasis on its long-term usefulness and do more research into it until they are superseded by something more modern.

Theorists of **NLP** are guilty of the same faults that are common in the fields of medicine and psychology. The findings that are founded upon facts, correlations, and case studies may lead to empirical conclusions which state that certain outcomes are predicted. The problem with this explanation is that it lacks an etiology, which is another word for a causal explanation. This indicates that assertions are being made despite the complete absence of any comprehension or relevant theory on the causes of the phenomena in question. This opens the door to the possibility that logical fallacies may emerge, and it also has the ability to stop or slow down the future expansion of intellectual capacity. The ANNH program is designed to make this situation better. Despite the fact that I believe there is a major chance to explain why the methods are effective, however, I highly doubt that my views will ever have an effect on the way that **NLP** training is delivered.

The Drawbacks Of Being A Manipulator

Manipulation must, of course, come with a few drawbacks or it wouldn't be called manipulation. If there weren't, then everyone would use this strategy all the time, and we wouldn't have some of the bad connotations that come with it along the road too. If there weren't, then everyone would use this strategy all the time. The downsides of this will manifest themselves most prominently either when you are not experienced enough in influencing others or when another person finds you in the process of manipulating them. As we go through each of these chapters, we will delve further into these topics. When you manipulate people or events in your life, you open yourself up to a variety of risks, including the following:

The act of manipulation is fraught with risk since it often results in unintended consequences. When another person is attempting to influence another person, that person's target will often have some form of sensation that the target is being manipulated. This is due to the fact that our awareness is raised to the concept that just because we desire something from another person, it is quite probable that someone else would want something from us as well. When a person becomes aware that they are being manipulated, it will not end well for you, and it will often cause a great deal of wrath, resentment, and other negative emotions.

Imagine that the target is aware that the manipulator is attempting to gain influence over them or that they have the feeling that the manipulator is attempting to gain some authority over them in a covert manner. In such a scenario, the target is quite unlikely to place any more faith in the aforementioned individual. If the target believes that they have been effectively manipulated at this stage, they may choose to withhold something from their manipulator as a means of exacting revenge. This may occur even if the goal that you are attempting to achieve is not very significant. And if the target believes that this manipulation has gone any farther and feels that their emotions are being played with, it is guaranteed to bring up a massive power struggle between the two individuals who are playing this game, and trust will fly out the window as a direct result of this.

Stimuli, limitations, and development are all intertwined.

Because even when we believe that our ideas do not influence the social, whether it be limited our way of seeing reality, this way we will have different attitudes that either restrict us or benefit us, thus contributing to both human development staff and community. So in order for us to have a better human development, we must first improve or change some of our neurolinguistic programming in order to have a better perspective of personal and social realities. Although we need to place a lot of emphasis on recognizing that we need to make some changes in our neurolinguistic programming in order for the fruit of our life to be determined by it, for instance: some people and communities are still living in extreme poverty as a direct result of having minds that are limited, fearful, lazy, or perhaps for cultural reasons remain limited to embark in a different way. This is the case despite the fact that we need to do a lot of work to recognize that we need to make these changes. Even when they recognize that their actions do not produce different outcomes, they still do not have the courage to try a new approach.

In this section, we will discuss what it is that we believe, who we are, and what the community believes and how that develops. We have come to realize that each of us relies on an ideological pattern in order to function more effectively, the brain increasingly setting new patterns of behavior that guide us to decide, act, and express who we are and how we feel, and in turn, these same patterns can be passed down from one generation to the next, which means that perhaps what our ancestors believed and decided is what we are basing our decisions and actions on. Therefore, in order to develop and acquire different and better outcomes each time, we need to examine and analyze our models of behavior and verify that they provide excellent results.

Continuing Education And Training

NLP training and coaching is increasingly popular in the business sector, where many companies and organizations are spending resources to teach their personnel in the NLP methods. These approaches promise higher productivity, which in turn leads to stronger bottom lines. NLP training and coaching is also quite popular in the entertainment industry. The following are some of the ways that neuro-linguistic programming (NLP) may assist you in improving your professional success:

1. You will be able to handle the management of people more effectively than you were able to do in the past, and you will be a more motivated leader overall.

2. You will be able to develop a strong relationship with your colleagues, employees, and subordinates, in addition to all of the other parties involved in your job.

3. You will be able to interact with the people at your job in a more efficient manner, ensuring that instructions and expectations are clearly conveyed and understood by everybody.

4. You will strengthen your presenting abilities and be able to persuade your audience, which will offer you a significant edge over other competitors.

5. The effectiveness of your meetings will improve in terms of producing goal-oriented action items that will maximize earnings and optimize the use of available resources.

6. You will be able to recognize and locate the appropriate individual to do

the appropriate task, so guaranteeing that the output of your whole commercial or professional endeavor is maximized in order to achieve the greatest possible outcomes.

7. You will be able to make greater use of problem-solving strategies, which will allow you to get the needed outcomes in a timely manner and with a minimum of fuss.

8. You will discover the courage and belief to overcome the hurdles of limiting ideas and outdated conceptions that are impeding the development and expansion of your organization. These barriers are holding your company back from reaching its full potential.

Your company or professional life will contain the following advantages as a result of the aforementioned benefits: enhanced productivity and enhanced efficiency

Better professional performance More resources to find solutions rather than wasting them on problems that appear to be insurmountable More motivated and contented employees, coworkers, and team members Staff growth and development Lower employee turnover More satisfied and happy customers A very healthy bottom line

Aspects of Sport

Techniques from the field of NLP are also being used by athletes to enhance their performance and significantly lower their levels of stress. The following is a list of some of the wonderful advantages that NLP methods provide in the field of sports:

1. As an athlete, you will be able to establish and accomplish objectives that are within your reach, which will both

boost your levels of motivation and improve the quality of your performance.

2. You will have the ability to transcend limiting thoughts and preconceived assumptions that are acting as obstacles in the way of your accomplishment.

3. You'll be able to draw from the deep well of energy that lies inside you. 4. You'll discover models in your industry and utilize their knowledge and experience to create your own competence. 5. You'll be able to network with others who share your interests.

In good health

Numerous studies have led researchers to the conclusion that using NLP methods may assist in the process of enhancing one's physical health. The following are some of the advantages that fall under this category:

1. You will notice a significant decrease in the amount of stress in your life.

2. You'll notice a considerable increase in the overall quality of your physical health.

3. You will discover that you have more energy in both your physical and mental systems if you rid your life of the kind of negativity that use a lot of energy.

4. You will discover the ability to cure yourself by using the power of your imagination.

5. You will have the opportunity to embrace ideas and practices that are beneficial to your overall health.

It makes a lot of sense to spend some amount of money in picking up these life-changing talents that can transform your personality for the better if you consider the extensive advantages that NLP training has for you. These skills can help you become a better version of yourself.

The Use Of NLP In Treatment And Beyond

Components of neuro-linguistic programming have applications in psychotherapy as well as other problem-solving contexts. It is possible to make life changes, find solutions to difficulties, and overcome obstacles with the aid of therapy. In addition to assisting those who are interested in personal growth, the Natural Language Processing (NLP) model teaches us to be more empathetic toward the experiences and perspectives of others and to comprehend the factors that motivate them. When used in therapy, NLP may assist with issues such as phobias, stress, sleeplessness, stuttering, or coping with intrusive ideas or compulsions. It also assists with the development of constructive habits and being more aware of one's emotions and thoughts so that they work with us rather than against us.

In this context, the modeling language is found to be highly beneficial, and therapists make use of it. It is important to keep in mind that non-verbal communication modeling (NLP) will not totally replace traditional psychotherapy; nonetheless, it may be of use to us, and as such, it need to be seen as an extra resource that can assist in the resolution of our issues and concerns. The knowledge gained through meta-programmes may also be valuable; it will allow us to communicate with our interlocutor more effectively and get a deeper understanding of the way that they think. The use of submodalities will result in improved thoughts and images, and they may also be of assistance in overcoming phobias or compulsions. Because NLP is a field that is always developing, the opportunities that it presents are almost limitless.

These methods are also used, for instance, in the process of employee training in order to personalize the educational experience and cater to the employees' specific requirements. The same is true when it comes to preparing a message for the interlocutor; if we are aware that the interlocutor displays, for instance, the qualities of a kinaesthetic, visual, or hearer, we are better able to tailor the message that will be presented to him or her. Therapeuts may make effective use of this information and then work toward altering the psychological aftereffects of, for instance, traumatic experiences from the client's past. However, when it comes to treatment, one of the essential components is collaboration with an expert. This part may be supplemented by consultation with an NLP practitioner or a coach, depending on the specifics of the situation.

The need for growth is present in every human being, but in some individuals, it is still very deeply buried. However, there is no question that everyone wants to be successful, and achieving even modest successes with the appropriate motivational system will unquestionably help one develop even further in their field and have a positive impact on their surroundings. In addition, NLP is used in the practice of mentoring, which, like the jobs of teaching and coaching, may be combined. The role of the coach is to give instruction and the development of suitable practices that promote learning and growth. The teacher is responsible for imparting new information. They frequently serve to define ideals, but most importantly, they help to set particular objectives, the efficacy and fulfillment of which are made more achievable owing to the employment of NLP procedures such as modeling or constructing a variety of models.

NLP strategies for establishing a goal support better planning, which in this case also includes, for instance, a career. This is something that any advisor working in a variety of disciplines would undoubtedly acknowledge. This particular field has long been acknowledged for the beneficial contributions it makes to the academic system, as well as to the management of work, the incentive to study, and other related areas. Everyone who puts in the effort to study or who applies their knowledge of NLP in conjunction with their understanding of psychology in their profession will unquestionably experience numerous advantages as a result. It is unquestionably worthwhile to make an effort to put one's understanding of neuro-linguistic programming to use in order to encourage others to engage in beneficial behaviors, to serve as a positive example to others, and to inspire them to grow personally and pursue their ambitions. Each of us has them buried deep inside us, and even if we are simply attempting to identify them correctly, using NLP methods will undoubtedly enable us to dig into them more quickly. These techniques will also most certainly assist us in planning our objective and achieving it.

www.ingramcontent.com/pod-product-compliance
Lightning Source LLC
Chambersburg PA
CBHW052144110526
44591CB00012B/1857